D1286949

www.finishinglinepress.com

A SKY FULL OF WINGS

New Women's Voices Series, No. 157

poems by

Ksenia Rychtycka

Finishing Line Press
Georgetown, Kentucky

A SKY FULL OF WINGS

New Women's Voices Series, No. 157

For My Family

ACKNOWLEDGMENTS

Grateful acknowledgment is made to the editors of the following
publications, in which versions of these poems originally appeared:

Alaska Quarterly Review: "Toward The Clear Blue Water"
Bear River Review: "Leaving Chicago" and "The Night We Knew Everything"
Hubbub: "When A Bird Flies Out Of The Sky And Into My Life"
The Literary Bohemian: "Train Ride To Zagreb" and "Why Honey Matters"
Mused Bella Online Literary Review: "When My Grandparents Left
Everything Behind" and "Watching Mother Return Home"
River Poems (An Anthology on The Allure Of Rivers): "A River Near
Chornobyl"
River Poets Journal (Featured Poet): "Acorns Like Bullets," "Only Rain,"
"Brushing Grandmother's Hair," "Bruge Repose With Laura," "Familiar
Ground," "When A Bird Flies Out Of The Sky And Into My Life"
The Writer's Guide/The Writer's Center: "Ode To Journeying"

Publisher: Leah Huete de Maines
Editor: Christen Kincaid
Cover Art: Edward (EKO) Kozak (Ukrainian, 1902-1992), News From
Ukraine, Oil on Canvas; Private Collection, Used by Permission. Photo by
Maria Bologna
Author Photo: Volodymyr Horobchenko
Cover Design: Elizabeth Maines McCleavy

Order online: www.finishinglinepress.com
also available on amazon.com

Author inquiries and mail orders:
Finishing Line Press
PO Box 1626
Georgetown, Kentucky 40324
USA

Table of Contents

*"And nothing seemed accidental because
it left traces on my heart."*
—*Lina Kostenko*

Ode To Journeying

If I could, I'd fly north to the land
of Midnight Sun. Wings outstretched,
I'd bob up and down, let wind toss me

and float through sky. Swim through clouds—
how hard could it be? If I could, I'd head
to my favorite overlooks where water crashes

down fjords and wooden stave churches
stand upright after hundreds of years.
Where night is light and sky alive—

swirling fireballs of green, red and blue.
I'd dance barefoot on Carpathian grass,
eye intricate eggs come to life at markets—

miniature fishes, horses, stags and deer
embraced by waves, circles, diamonds—
smallest triangles nestled in palm of my hand.

If I could, I'd jump aboard a Viking longship,
sail up the Dnipro river, breath let loose as waves—
rhythm of oars lulling me to fly.

The endless sky above.

HOME

Leaving Chicago

Red is the crash
of my first bike, sprawled,
no longer urgent, forgotten
outside my childhood home.

Still, it would have just been
another day, my brother chasing
me round the plastic pool, garden
hose sputtering, bare feet
sliding on porch steps.

Can you hear the fervent whispers
of the house half-purged? Wallpaper
slipping from corner to linoleum
floor and still the cat awaits
its morning milk.

Mother floats from neighbor's house
to backyard stoop, running fingers
over bared clotheslines, no more crumbs
for her sparrows, birdbath run dry.

Father likes open sky, vast
stretches of time where his
taptaptap of words slices deep—
as a felled tree crushed to its core.

Uncle scolds my brother, talks of darkening
sky, wasted moments as we run then hide
among boxes of chipped dishes, hand-painted
tea set shipped direct from New York City.

We peer into the cherry curio cabinet,
staid backdrop where Mother and Father pose
in their finest evening wear—buttoned
evening gloves and silk pocket square.

Glam Hollywood couple with smiles held tight,
eyes unblinking as ice.

Watching Mother Return Home, 1990

Steady rain, then a light mist clings
to the window as blurs of flowered
windowboxes and grazing goats soar past.
The train from Budapest to Lviv runs fast,
then slow, hiccupping to a stop.

Arrival is delayed. Half a century gone by
and Mother waits to touch Ukrainian ground,
slip into the reverie of a childhood
half-remembered, dreams of teaching
in rural mountain villages never quashed.

Six hours go by as new wheels are fitted
onto the wider tracks slashing East
from West—orders of Stalin—
an iron fist clasped shut.

In last miles, the railcar thunders
over coarse earth covering unmarked
graves. Outside there are green mountains,
a lightening sky, whispering wind
nudging Mother from her seat as she rises,

stretching her arms out like wings.

When My Grandparents Left Everything Behind

There wasn't much Petro could fit
in the wagon after Anna

and the children clambered
into the back, brown mare

leading them west past wooden church,
schoolhouse and the little footbridge

where he'd stroked Anna's hair
for the first time, hand shaking.

Oh—the absurd joy of youth,
the house he'd built still a dream

in his heart. Now his beloved bees
were in old Danylo's care. They'd be back

in Roznitiv in a few weeks, Petro promised, two
months at most. The wagon lumbered over dirt

roads, high into the green Carpathians, away
from familiar words and creeks, a few gold coins

and jars of honey packed tightly inside.

Familiar Ground

When Mother drops to the ground, kissing
the earth, even wind takes notice and stills

its breath. Sunflowers lie limp in waiting children's
arms while the train conductor claps and claps,

discarded tickets lying crumpled beneath his feet.
Mother, no longer the shy child who hid

behind her braids, falls into an embrace of strangers
as my brother and I count heads, then look

for familiar smiles in unfamiliar faces—
Dido's toothy grin, that piercing blue of Babtsia's eyes.

Yet one man stands apart, shuffling
worn shoes in hot dirt, face bleached as holiday linen.

Mother's three brothers lost on this ancestral land.
Forty-seven years swallowed whole.

One man staggers forward.
Two cousins reunite.

With Father, Mother danced the tango, fast
as gunshots once chasing her across Europe.

Here, Mother treads slow—pointed toes
and stiffened arms—relearning first steps

on native soil.

What I Remember

I am perhaps two. Our house is still.
Only almond refrigerator hums.

Through second-floor windows,
afternoon sun skips over kilim rug.

Barefoot and happy, I run over,
jump on its red and green zigzags.
.
Oblivious, Father naps on the sofa.
Such a rare treat to see him home.

Draftsman by day, bus driver by night.
Author in moments of in-between.

I push away embroidered pillows, hands
insistent on Father's back till he wakes,

pulls me close. We are as snug as birds
nesting. Soon our nest will empty.

Soon he will be gone.
For now, I hold on tight.

I Knew Nothing

After the '67 blizzard in Chicago,
my older sister and brother pulled
me on a sled. Mountains of white
encroached on all sides—
the crunch of snow, ice melting
on my tongue. Mother waved
from the steps while Father's coat
pockets bulged with chocolate
as he trudged to work.

That spring, daffodils burst out
in sweet symmetry. Our street blazed
yellow. Father gave me a watering can.
Mother stayed inside.

That summer we moved to Detroit
while the city burned. Father stayed
behind. At three, I knew nothing
of lament. Of the breaking of family.
Of fires ravaging homes, neighborhoods—
the unbidden force of change

that swoops down. Again and again.

JOURNEYING

Backpacking Europe

This is what I miss—train rushing past castles
and farmlands. Stone circles. Black sand of Perissa

warm against my feet. Greek stranger singing out
an open window. Exploring ruins at Tintagel with Lila,

my soft-spoken childhood friend who saved a pigeon,
yet years later, couldn't save herself.

Road maps were not my strength though I did well enough
in most cities, navigating canals and twisty streets, living

in hostels and on houseboats, thin mattress strewn
across floors in Grindelwald, Bath and Brussels.

At twelve at scout camp, I trudged on desolate trails,
green backpack crushing my spine. The lilt of Ukrainian songs.

Back then I was always a pace behind my friends—
out of step, out of tune. Later I learned to keep abreast

with shifting sky, friendly bicyclists, Swiss septuagenarians
who never stopped for air.

How breathless those stark cliffs of fjords, stained glass of Chartres.
How surprised Lila was when I found her asleep, hidden

in a sea of backpacks just outside Munich after we'd split off
to explore different countries, our lives unfettered.

We hugged each other in that city where I lost my way
day after day, heading uptown instead of downtown,

east mimicking west, wind squealing in my ears.
And how those crows cackled—sky full of wings.

Bruges Repose With Laura

Surely you remember that day—
handful of Belgian baguette, chunk
of cheese and all those cameras

dancing stern to bow. First clouds
then water lilies. Stone bridge
as centerpiece—cobbled pathway

and sun more dazzling than the crystal
earrings swinging from my ears.
That boat ride seemed to last for hours,

our laughter sweet as Droste chocolates
the staring Dutch man tried to bribe
us with in return for some conversation.

We were in no mood to talk. Not with
twenty years unbridled like rapids.
Not with untrod trails all around.

How we loved it all—the medieval square,
the boy playing the harpsichord,
lovely music and lovely lips

though he spared neither of us a second
glance. That day we rebuffed
chocolate and embraced the sky.

Pinpricks. A lazy afternoon.
And then it was gone.

Only Rain

Lila's neck thrown back at a slant
reminds me of those swans in Heidelberg
as they glided across rippled shadows.

A picture's all I can touch now yet I still hear
our smothered giggles as we clamped fingers
over lips tightly, hiding in leafy arms

of the neighbor's tree. We felt giddy and safe.
Just two kids running through the apple orchard—
our deserted battlefield where British and German

spies we'd conjured on the page hunched
behind cornstalks on nearby farms.

Years later, I recall Lila sitting curbside in Brussels,
soothing a pigeon who'd crash-landed
into ground. I waited for her that time

although I longed to sightsee, take pictures
of the Manneken-Pis, shop for scarves
in smallest of shops. She gazed in windows.

I ran ahead. It rained hard in Tintagel
one night. Lila wanted to sit alone.
That night there were no tears.

Only rain.

Travelers

Waves smash
onto jagged peaks
at Land's End
as we sit silently
before evening
storms strike.

We backpack
through Cornwall,
pose near crumbling
castles, crawl through
stone circles in search

of magic—our childhood
fantasies unearthed
like long-buried
pottery shards.

Our smiles are fresh
as starched dresses
pulled hot
from under the iron.

Whistling trains
carry us to Salisbury,
Oxford, Bruges,
Heidelberg and on.

We bask in a symphony
of foreign words—
first brash, then soft
and sweet to our ears

until months later,
the screech of plane wheels
jolts us back to home
and we are ordinary
once again.

Train Ride To Zagreb

Love boards the train in Salzburg,
stumbles along a dim corridor
like tumbling clowns
I cowered from
at the three-ring circus.

It's my door love finally falls
through—how my face burns—
is it innocence or envy
when middle-aged lovers
don't even spare me a glance
in an otherwise-empty compartment?

Apparently love has no boundaries
or need of hastily contrived disguises.

This love is bound to fail I think
at the border of Yugoslavia, fragile
as the country that's about to split
its seams, one man waving his hat
in farewell, one woman braiding snips
of light and dark for a locket
she has yet to buy.

Not far from Zagreb, a wife
readies her bags, a husband gives
away a bouquet of wilted daisies
to the little girl who's tripped
over station steps and dirtied
her embroidered dress.

Not far from Zagreb, a woman speaks
of infidelities and I dream of longings
I have yet to bear.

Toward The Clear Blue Water

On this island, streets run crooked
as old women, their smiles cracked—
broken bits of tooth and gaps that stop
no one, only entice me closer till I see
the curves of their backs have taken on
the geography of their locale.

Like the misshapen tree left standing
in the wake of a thunderstorm
and in the clear morning after
as debris lines sides of road—
stubs of doll arm, leg, glossed-over lips
stick out from shards of glass.

It's not anyone's fault these women's hands
are gnarled as paths crisscrossing
this island, their worn smiles stuck to skin.
They've seen hundreds stomp

past their doorsteps toward clear blue
water and sand sparkling so bright
no one notices the old women's hands
circling, yarn so pliant in their touch, soft
as sun's descent.

Remembering The Oracle

Alone on a bus from Athens to Delphi,
the road coils like a snake.
I've never been big on thrill rides
yet my driver delights in taunting
other roadsters, giving no ground
on narrow lanes.

The Oracle awaits. Here Pythia—
priestess who breathed in vapors
from crevices in earth, then mumbled
cryptic words to those seeking answers
about love, war and everything in between—
doled out words of counsel.

One blazing-hot day,
I wander through hilly terrain
to stand before an ancient temple.
Sacred spring. Sacred earth. Sacred shrine.

I've brought no gifts for Pythia, follower
of Apollo—Greek god of divination.
Instead I sprinkle pebbles on this soil
deemed to be the navel of the world
and look for clues to my future.

Once home in Detroit, two rolls of film
turn up blank. Not even a shadow to hint
of the Oracle I visited that day, postcard
of temple ruins I'd bought at kiosk lost
on a Yugoslavian train.

Three decades on and stuck in evening
traffic, I sip iced latte, restless preteen
daughter at my side. I start to speak but stop,
bouzouki music pulsating on car radio,

my child of little words swaying in delight
to the unfamiliar taste of Greek words—
taking me back to Pythia—when no answer
proved to be the true answer.

ANCESTRAL LAND

River Near Chornobyl

This still river sparkles
with the luster of a life well-lived,
the best wine saved for banqueting hour
at a table carved from tallest oak. I walk
along its bank, peer at ghost silhouettes
of thousand-year-old Viking ships
once plying this waterway from barren north
to the gold domes of a city decked in splendor.

At a nearby café, the locals speak in sing-song.
A woman licks her chocolate ice cream cone,
tells me of flames bouncing high, villagers
clamped to sidewalks like lampposts—
watching a nuclear reactor burn to the sky.
Locals danced at two weddings that night.
Her cone falls to the ground:

"No one told us to leave.
Not for another two days."

Midday sun heats the riverbank as I climb
aboard a sightseeing cruise. This river is still
and sparkles like the finest jewel.
Yet the river weeps in places far beyond
the bends of easy reach and camera's eye—
somewhere far below the swirl of a wave
tossing up boats high and fast.

When A Bird Flies Out Of The Sky And Into My Life

You'll think it's silly, but let me tell you
when a lime-green bird flew onto my Kyiv
balcony, things changed for the better.

It wasn't as though dark sky shifted
into that summer blue of lazy bicycle rides
where, long ago, I sat on my teen neighbor's

handlebars, breathing in an orange lily
he plucked from his mother's garden and pinned
to my blouse. After all, it was mid-December.

That bird's singing coaxed me out of my flat,
coaxed me out of soft slippers and ragtag robe.
If I believed in omens, I would have unbraided

my hair and patted some rouge onto my cheeks.
I would have danced tip-toe across balcony,
my mouth filled with sudden hope of sun.

Instead I opened my door wide to the sky,
colored gray as old promises. Stubborn bird
refused to leave even as I teased with whispers

of lush gardens if he'd just fly farther south.
But when he swooped down on my shoulder,
I saw nothing more than one lost stray

come to warm the soul of another.
My door was open and the sky was sad.
Maybe for both of us, it was as simple as that.

The Night We Knew Everything

For Volodya

That night, we walked the cracked sidewalks
of the city you were born in—Kyiv,

city I fell in love with years earlier
and thousands of miles away, while sitting

in a Saturday school classroom, tracing
photo edges of golden domes, wide-eyed mosaics,

and don't forget the legend about the three brothers
and their sister Lybid—Kyiv's legendary founders.

She is the river I wanted to swim even then,
current strong as a wall of stones.

That night we decided it all even as we held hands
and kept our words unformed. Who needed to speak

against touch of skin, night bright with full moon?
We laughed in spite of slapping wind, followed streets

winding over old merchant pathways.
A thousand years of dirt crunched beneath our shoes.

We cared only for the present, familiar
as the strays that roamed Khreshchatyk, the granite

statue of three brothers and their sister on a longship,
Lybid perched on the prow, ready to take flight.

Did we believe in that city legend? The wandering
brothers and sister who came long ago and set up camp

on these hilly slopes. Kyi, Schek, Khoryv, Lybid.
City, two hills and a river named for each sibling.

Perhaps they did for a time, then packed
their traveling bags—took along smoked

deer meat and set out in search of new adventures,
lush mountain range, the sweetest of wine.

Or perhaps they were born here, as children carved
out hideways in overgrown birch and evergreens.

Who knows if the city you are born in will remain
the city you grow old with—in spirit if not flesh?

But that night was ours, the promise of flight still ahead,
future certain as ancient earth beneath our feet.

Visiting Drohobych

Newly engaged, we arrive spontaneously
in Father's birthplace near the Carpathians,
laughing as the Soviet-era Tavria jolts us

over broken roads. A trip to celebrate our
engagement, sip coffee in downtown square
where Father raced cousins over cobblestones,

book bag slung over shoulder. Nearly two decades
since Father's been gone. Only now can I walk
his city, tour splendid 15th-century timbered church—

masterpiece of folk art filled with frescoes.
We are greeted by scaffolding set against gleaming
wood and octagonal domes. No workers there. No way in.

Instead we wander narrow streets and bicker—
over timetables, asking for directions—sidestepping
one another's dark looks till we stumble into a random

print shop, bright-eyed proprietor rising to his feet,
ecstatic to see new faces and proffer assortments
of chocolate, then tea. *How about shots of cognac?*

Apparently, Father's hometown connection
makes us family. We learn there is a street that bears
my family name. It's as much a surprise as the dawn

phone call that came all those years ago—Uncle stammering
on the line in grief. For seconds, Mother—blurry-eyed,
mistook his voice for Father's—*Lubko, is that you?*

Later, posing under the street sign, I recall Father's final visit
to Detroit, his first grandchild nestled in his arms, lost years
shuffled underfoot as we all came together one last time.

Watching A Revolution From A Computer Screen
Ukraine, 2014

Drone of drum, hand over hand,
beat for beat, breath for breath.

Silence as much an illusion as the snake
charmer who plays it up for the crowd.

Slightest curve of hand—he thinks you're fooled.
Let the snake loose, unfurl the fury.

The coffers have long been bare.
These streets, your streets, my streets

are now covered in blood. What can we do—
here, now—as black tires flare?

Even the poet has been pummeled.
The screen darkens and still we watch.

CIRCLE OF LIFE

Grandfather Revealed

Dido Petro cracked walnuts when he was happy,
sitting at the head of the ornate oak table,

smoking Kent cigarettes even when his fingers
curled inward from the same arthritis that curved

Babtsia's back. He was feisty and unapologetic,
had no time for family who'd arrive late

to Christmas Eve dinner, never mind the tire gone flat
or icy roads. I treaded carefully when his moods changed,

played quietly with my dolls on the brown, slipcovered
sofa, chatted with imaginary friends on front porch

steps and counted moments until Mother arrived
to take me home. Dido's good moods were harder to come by

once Babtsia died, but he'd surprise me from time to time,
ask me to tea and then we'd talk about tulips blooming

in his front yard, the times he'd taken me and my brother
to the state fair, how I'd gone flying down the superslide,

yellow braids swinging through air, the noisy bus ride
downtown. Yet Dido never talked about the journey

that brought him all the way from Ukraine to Detroit,
the journal he'd kept when he'd fled his homeland,

the bomb that almost killed his family while they
huddled under an oak tree.

His journal tells me stories that Dido never could,
how his eldest boy Myron snuck out at night and ran off

to fight with the partisans. At just 17, did his steps falter outside?
Did Myron imagine he'd never again wake up to the smell

of his mother's borsch, taste honey gathered from Dido's beloved
bees? Could he imagine his father's lament:

Oh, my child, if you knew how much your family longs to see you,
you would fly to us from the farthest corners.

Brushing Grandmother's Hair

Babtsia wasn't the sort of woman who'd swoon
over a smart new dress or latest shade of starlet's lipstick—
Ava Gardner and Liz Taylor be damned.

No jewelry chest would make her happy after she'd lost
first one, then two, then three of her sons.
I wasn't around when her dark hair hung low

down her back, when Dido tended his bees like beloved
children. They were long gone when I set foot in Roznitiv,
ancestral home of peeling gray paint and overgrown shrubs

greeting me like their wayward dog lost in panic of military
convoys and gunfire. In the village graveyard, I hunched
over faded headstones amid wildflowers gone mad.

Searched for names of their little boys but only found a turkey
who chased me down the dirt path. Babtsia was stooped over
by the time I got to meet her, not too fond of how I twirled

around the living room and plopped down on her embroidered
pillows. At seven, front porch steps became my escape
as I plotted Pippi Longstocking-like adventures, played

with my brother's colored marbles. Once, Babtsia took out
her sewing machine and made dresses for my Barbie dolls,
then let me slip on buttoned silk gloves that I'd never seen her wear.

She never told me stories about her childhood. Or how she'd fled
her homeland. How she'd crouched beside her children's graves,
swept dirt from their headstones, sat on cold ground for hours.

No—Babtsia wasn't much of a talker but the day she called
out to me at dawn, her voice loomed so loud I grew afraid.
Braids undone, I brushed and brushed her gray hair.

Can't say my fingers didn't shake or her hair was silky,
but I'll never forget her broad smile, the fierce grip
of her arms, an unexpected embrace.

Slippage

I read aloud to Mother,
enunciating her own words—
the poems she'd stayed up
nights writing after years alone
raising children—velvet
night her muse, her savior.

Mother smiles but sits mute,
stroking my palm. Blue eyes
wander. Already I am losing her.
She wants to go back to her
childhood home in Roznitiv,
live with her mother and father
long gone.

I distract her—sing off-key,
folk songs we once twirled to
on the linoleum floor of our
compact kitchen, feet stomping
with passion of Hutsul mountain
folk or young couples jumping
bonfires on Midsummer Eve.

Mother hums along, happy.
These songs are in her bones.
These songs have traveled
through blood-stained lands—
sustained her through bombings
and a rough ocean crossing
taking her far—then farther still
from her childhood home.

Mother doesn't know of the current
war in her homeland, of one hundred
protesters shot dead by snipers
on same square where we danced
on New Year's Eve, of Crimea overrun
on Kremlin's orders, of soldiers
slipping over the Ukrainian border seventy
years after she'd fled all those invaders.

No, Mother doesn't know.
And if only for this—
I am glad.

Why Honey Matters

I (1944)

Back in Ukraine, Dido loved beekeeping.
Behind barbed wire at an internment camp,
his honey bought bread for Mother, Uncle
and Babtsia. Every crumb prized.
Each morsel gulped. Always aching for more.

II (2018)

Mother comes to me as I'm making honey cake,
measuring out sugar then whipping eggs.
Never mind that Mother left this earth
eighteen months earlier. I can sense her pleasure,
her presence—palpable as smoke.

I apologize aloud for running out of buckwheat
honey which we both know tastes best. Dark
as amber—flavored like musk and molasses.
But Mother doesn't mind. In my empty kitchen,
I sense no disapproval.

Now that Mother's with me, I grow bold
with my spices. Extra ginger and cinnamon.
Grated orange rind. Splash of rum.
Like Mother, I don't hold back.

III (1990)

First boil honey. Then cool it.
But don't get lax. Boiled too long,
honey loses its essence.

Great-Aunt whispers in my ear
after too much Crimean Muscat—
table laden with cheese, kovbasa, crepes,
thick slices of seven-layered honey cake—
one layer for each decade she's lived.
Homemade cherry wine slips down my throat.

It's been 47 years since Great-Aunt last
embraced Mother. This morning, in Carpathian
hometown—a blue door opened. Tremor
of hands. Rush of feet. No words spoken.
Only the chirping of birds outside.
Only the caress of reunion inside.

For The Child Who Doesn't Speak

Only child. Gentle as first speck
of dawn. Outside your bedroom window
wind becomes your friend.
The fiercer autumn leaves sway,
the louder your glee.

When you were born our world sashayed
into bloom—branches teeming
with purple and white, scent of lilac
welcoming us home. We became three.

Dizzy from sleepless nights,
dark blurring into light—
I whispered stories in your ear
then watched your father rock
you to slumber.

More than a decade later, the words
you cannot express float toward us
and somehow we understand and nod,
urging a little more, a tad louder, clearer.
We are greedy for all that you can give.

On the trampoline you are poised like a bird,
an instant to momentum. Hands stretched out—
you sense new possibility. Our eyes meet
and then you rise higher than I can reach,
my arms cradling only air.

Acorns Like Bullets . . .

pelt the swing set
where my daughter plays,
clapping her hands
and raising them high.
You can't compress her mad joy,
belly laughs like thunder, small
feet pounding on damp ground.
Our yard's a combat zone when
acorns come crashing down, chipped
and broken—no time to dive for cover,
not even a quick look at bloated clouds.

The sun slinks just above the neighbor's
oaks—portending the arrival of a helicopter
that buzzes overhead and stills, circling
above our yard, an endless stretch
of whirring blades and searching eyes
that at last fade into sky.

I think of that warplane from some seventy
years ago, hovering over the giant oak
where Babtsia fell faint and Dido clutched
Mother and Uncle in his arms. Mother
never remembered the way Dido described
these moments in his journal, how close
that aircraft swung to ground—pilot's face visible
through cockpit window—one family of four
against one pilot's mercy.

The endless sky above.

Additional Acknowledgments

I am very appreciative to the following poets and organizations: The Bear River Writer's Conference (Richard Tillinghast), Poetry Forge and The Interlochen Center For The Arts (Holly Wren Spaulding), The Kentucky Women Writer's Conference (Bianca Lynne Spriggs), Poetry Barn (Lissa Kiernan and Judith Roney), and The Writer's Center (Meg Eden).

I'm especially grateful to poet and essayist Laura Bernstein-Machlay for her invaluable input and many years of friendship. Special thanks to my fellow authors who have deeply inspired and encouraged me over the years: Myrosia Stefaniuk, Dorene O'Brien, Olenka Kalytiak Davis, Natalia Iwanyckyj Tegler and Nina Orlovskaya. Much appreciation to Chrystyna Kozak and the entire Kozak family for usage of the Edward Kozak painting. Deep thanks and love to my husband Volodya and daughter Lina, and the entire Rychtyckyj, Slywynsky and Sirota clan for their endless support.

Edward ("EKO") Kozak (1902-1992) was a renown Ukrainian artist, cartoonist, illustrator, writer, editor and publisher. He was born in the village of Hirne in the Carpathian foothills of western Ukraine. He studied art in Vienna, Lublin and Lviv at the noted Oleksa Novakivsky Art School, known for its artistic innovation. In 1949, he immigrated to the United States and settled in Detroit, Michigan, where he worked as an animator in television films. As an artist he utilized different mediums, such as oils, gouache, acrylics and mosaics. He was prolific and created over 700 paintings during his years in the United States. Thematically, his paintings highlighted his Ukrainian heritage— bygone village life and traditions, the colorful lore and life of the Hutsuls (pastoral highlanders inhabiting regions of the Carpathian Mountains), as well as heroic episodes in the struggle for Ukrainian independence. He is also well-known for his book illustrations, illustrations for Ukrainian folk songs, folk sayings and superstitions, and his satirical yet good-natured caricatures.

Sources: The Ukrainian Museum: "Introducing Artists from The Ukrainian Museum's Fine Art Collection," Facebook post, January 21, 2021; Wolynetz, Lubow. "A Gift of Twenty-Two Edward Kozak Paintings," The Ukrainian Museum and Library of Stamford, January 2, 2014.

Ksenia Rychtycka is a first-generation Ukrainian-American poet and fiction writer. She has a Master of Arts degree in Creative Writing from Columbia College Chicago and a Bachelor of Arts degree in Journalism with a minor in art history from Wayne State University. Ksenia worked as an editor in Ukraine during the early years of the post-Soviet era, an experience which has inspired her creative work.

Her poetry, fiction and feature articles have appeared in numerous literary journals, anthologies and periodicals. She was a Featured Poet in *River Poets Journal* and has received honorable mentions for her poetry in the 45th New Millennium Writing Awards and the Rochester Writers Margo Lagattuta Award Contest. Her short story collection, *Crossing The Border*, was a finalist in the 2013 Next Generation Indie Book Awards. She was also selected as a finalist in the Blue Mesa Review Fiction Contest and the 2020 New Women's Voices Chapbook Competition.

Ksenia has participated in literary presentations of her work at the Cornelia Street Café in New York City and Ukrainian-American Writers: A New Generation of Literary Voices at the Ukrainian Institute of Modern Art in Chicago. She has backpacked through twelve countries in Europe, and after sojourns in Chicago and Kyiv, Ukraine, resides with her family in the Detroit metro area where she was raised.

In 2020, Ksenia was awarded a spot in the inaugural Historical Fiction Masterclass (organized by the Historical Novel Society), where she began working on a new project. Visit her website at kseniarychtycka.com.

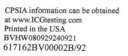

9 781646 626151